Sleeve Heart

Eleanor May Blackburn

Stairwell Books //

Published by Stairwell Books
161 Lowther Street
York, YO31 7LZ

www.stairwellbooks.co.uk
@stairwellbooks

Sleeve Heart © 2025 Eleanor May Blackburn and Stairwell Books

All rights reserved. No part of this publication may be reproduced, stored in or introduced into a retrieval system, or transmitted, in any form, or by any means (electronic, mechanical, photocopying, recording, e-book or otherwise) without the prior written permission of the author.

The moral rights of the author have been asserted.

ISBN: 978-1-917334-09-9

Illustrated by Clara Sims

'Being broken up with by a mediocre white guy isn't as bad as a brain injury'- *Caitlin Blackburn 2022*

Table of Contents

Breaking	1
Roll up roll up, broken artist for sale (name your price)	2
All the fun but it doesn't feel fair	4
Heart Break for fucks sake	5
Organs that I have inside me	7
The one that was too much	9
Cheap	11
Stating the obvious	12
So much	13
Happy	15
A funny concept	16
Alien thing	17
A stranger	19
Untitled 1	21
Untitled 2	22
Boring	23
You just got rejected	24
ROMP	27
Sleepless	28
Bare	31
#1 of #2	32
square peg	34
Hum (in my) Drum	35
Untitled 3	36
Untitled 4	37
Untitled 5	38
Travelling	39
Mardy Bum	40
Blissful ignorance	43
Going higher	44
Apart	46
You've never known anxiety until //	47
The artist that knows	48
I had a lot of time but at the same time no time at all	50

London 1 and 2	51
Leeds 1 and 2	52
Birmingham 1 and 2	53
Oh York oh York	54
People of Edinburgh that made an impression	55
A cream place called home	56
Loving	58
Let's go girls	59
Gathering	62
Recipe for a reyt good day out	63
SPL IT	65
Strange behaviour	67
Meet me in the pumpkin patch	68
Learn and remember	69
We go to Tenerife in under a month	70
Kittens	72
Baff	73
Untitled 6	74
Untitled 7	75
Untitled 8	76
Untitled 9	77
In another life you squeezed me out to fill out the donuts	78

Breaking

I relate my life to *Sex and the City*
Much more frequently
Than I'd like to
For a girl with her heart on her sleeve
What else is there to do

Roll up roll up, broken artist for sale (name your price)

Why do we have to sell our souls to prove that our art matters? I'm selling mine, synapse by sinew, and it's leaving my withering carcass in tatters. The question scatters: what's next, what's best, say it with your chest. How can you top that? A brain injury, sexual anxiety, and another type of anxiety got me feeling crap. Further projects got me reeling, so inside I'm screaming, outside I'm perplexed. The lady doth protest too much, but I'm possessed by always needing to be better, there's no other way I'm gonna feel better, so maybe if I just do better and write better and speak better and look better and hurt more and be sore and fuck war, but let's write about it and fuck sexism but let's talk about it and racism can fuck right off, but who am I to shout about it?

Cos, please, we're all burning our bodies just to get a good grade in our motherfucking degrees. And dropping LSD not for fun but to see what art is the outcome and then baring it for all to see. But at what cost? What are we playing at selling our souls? Without even steady payrolls and the one that controls it all doesn't give a fuck and our so-called goals are always pretty fucked up. You wouldn't say I'm mentally healthy and us artists are not typically wealthy - by that I mean we're poor as shit but we'd do anything just to get that hit from the stage from the page to the produced to the publisher at the expense of our wellbeing. I'm constantly working and when I'm not I hit rock bottom and I'm on a come down from the work in question. I feel stressed and shitty giving my art, I mean, fuck, it's so hard and after I've rode the tiny high, I feel even more stressed and shitty not giving it. I'm essentially addicted to the Avant Garde.

So yeah, it's hard but if you don't have a story it's even harder. 99% perspiration 1% inspiration, so why do those without a sob story not make it past graduation? If you manage to without, you know you're scraping. Trauma comes with adoration, admiration despite the classic degradation- if you've not got something terrible to say, no one's gonna listen. Life experience - I've got plenty of that - more labels than you can throw a shitty stick at. And what shitty sticks they are. Maybe I should be grateful for my trauma. I know many people are. But here's an idea: how about we stop working like dogs drooling over bones (sometimes our own but more likely someone else's) just a little out of our reach, that someone's gonna kick away anyway when they realise, we don't have a story worthy of a decent speech. Freedom of speaking, trauma dumping, free trauma speeching. Yeah, I'm lucky I nearly died.

All the fun but it doesn't feel fair

I didn't understand how the jealousy of my younger self is like candy floss.

Baby pink like my blushing cheeks, flushed with gentle anger at my former youth and beauty.

Much too sweet, far sweeter than now, for all the things I didn't know then.

Fairground rides that forced me to throw up all down my stiff, ironed, purple jeans.

Nostalgia and melancholic tunes hitting me square in the jaw.

Sadness for the past in the present.

Let me gobble it all up until my teeth rot and fall out one by one from the sickening sugar.

Gummy and lacking smiles in more ways than one.

Heart Break for fucks sake

I may still be on standby
But today
I didn't even cry

Today I did
My eyes puffy and swollen
Too small for their giant sockets

Today I waited and waited
Video icon flashing
I closed my app
It was a glitch

I dreamt so many times it happened
One day I woke up and it did

I knew it'd be difficult

I didn't realise quite how much
What it was like to not want you?
I can't remember
This too will pass
But god I wish it would pass quickly

Something finally makes me laugh
I go to tell
I can't-

Something makes me cry
I go to tell
Never mind
Something makes me scream
I want to tell
I forget

All it took was one week to unravel
Just one
Tortured visceral heart-wrenching week
It's rather shocking
How fast happiness
Can be stripped away

Organs that I have inside me
(Originally published in Full House Lit)

See how it twists and turns in my gut
Churning my long and small intestines up
Blending my pancreas, liver and stomach
Fixing my mouth in a sickly lucid curve of a smile
It takes more muscles to frown than to smile
It takes almost the same to frown and to smile
Frown and smile in perfect damage
Fleshy mouth organ always at the top
Means something I think
So you are told
I stare at the funny lumps and bumps of the blushing flesh in a piece of glass
Mirror doesn't reflect the truth
Yes
NO
I wash my hands again to be safe
Taking care not to look up
Don't want to see that
Laura phoned just for a chat
Don't want to talk
My gut bubbles and pops like a cork
Plastering red entrails along the walls
Let's paint the town crimson
My bedroom hardly counts as town
I have worms in my feet and butterflies in my belly and grasshoppers raving inside my skull
I could snap like a twig

But the sound would reverberate
off the wine-coloured walls and-
Take off
I could melt/I could fly/I could fall/I could rise/I could fly/
I could fall
I could fall
I could fall
I could fall
I could fall
I could fall

I could –

My heart leaps straight out of my concaved chest

The one that was too much

Fuck

I just wanted a cup of tea
But that mug reminds me
Of you and me
The one with the cats all over
That I would always use
To make your morning cuppa
Your mug- really
That's the toothpaste we bought together
When we went on a York trip
And had nothing to brush our peggies with
Unlike the time
Only a few weeks ago
We stayed at Joe's
And brushed teeth with fingers
And we kissed
Two foam covered noses
Here's another pair of socks
You gave me to cover my eternally ice-cold toes
I'm accidentally on purpose
Still sleeping in your t-shirt
On my dressing table a picture
Of us at the dungeons together
This is scarier
When I load my laptop you're there
After being forced into a photograph
Because I got the face on

My favourite earrings were from you
And my favourite jumper too
Every beep on my phone
Gives me hope for a second
That I won't die alone
Alas - just another spam email
I am constantly in tears
I don't know what else to do
Even now I'm writing about you
Ignoring all the things I should do
In the hope that in a few weeks
When this all blows over
I can show you
You'll laugh and poke fun
"Oh, you"
Instead I'll just be silently
Picking my fingers
Wondering where/ how/ what
 You're up to

Cheap

When I first paraded
The heart-shaped bruise
Lining my almost translucent throat
I was told
By a family friend
I looked cheap
I was embarrassed
Confused
How can love be *cheap*
So we began to cover private places
Building shadows in unseen special spaces
We planted them on skin that was shy
Until we were littered as clouds in a stormy sky
For a short while
Then
Cheap crept back in
Now I keep my love even more quiet
So not even I can see it
And I don't call it

Love anymore

Stating the obvious

      "Why do you have spaghetti on your face?"
"Because I like spaghetti"
so
      "Why do you have heartbreak on your face?"
"Because he left"

      "Help me please, I'm having a heart attack"
"No, you're just having a break up."
      "I don't know who I am without him"
"You will."
      "I'll never feel OK again"
"Unfortunately, you will."

"I want to hurt myself"
"I want to die"
"I'm dying"
         "Get some self-respect."
"I needed to hear that"

So much

YOU'RE THE ONLY THING I LIKE
Really
I'd snog that smile straight off your face
The one that reveals your little chip
Makes you even more
Perfect
I do that quite a lot
Actually
Maybe because I don't know what to say most of the time
How do you have a conversation with someone
So much more
But
Do you feel much for me
You say all the right things
Of course you do
I'd be upset if you didn't
But would you be upset
If I Ended things
Would you grieve
Would you demolish a tub of ice cream
Would you cry to your friends
Watch shit tv
Because
I don't think you would
I think you'd move on

And pretty quickly too

And it makes me feel good
That you'd still feel good
Hardly pausing to not feel good
But
At the same time
I want you to grieve me
I want it to tear at your insides and make you feel
Dreadful
Not that I want you to feel dreadful
Most of the time
Nearly all the time
This is the exception
Does that make me terrible
The wicked witch of the west
I want you to love me yes
And you often prove as such
With evidence
And facts
And statistics
And others
suitable to your entirely gracious characteristics
But I want you to need me more
Someone
me
So much

Happy

my happy pills regulate my mood !!
keep me shovelling food !
so I'm calmer
and fatter
they keep me tired
so I don't have energy to be sad
and even if I did
I'd not be able to get drunk about it
without passing out
can't do without them
but don't function with them
I mean obviously
I do to the outside eye
- inwardly ??
I'm not even here
I'm beginning to forget
If
I
ever
w a   s

A funny concept

Imagination is a funny thing
A not always sunny thing
Plays tricks and torments
In the dead of night
So you can't sleep tight enough
Plagued by ghosts and ghouls
Or perhaps just my
Incessant shivering touch
Please hold me tighter
But not as tight as your perfect -
While we are stoned and singing
I sit on the bed wrapped in a towel
My thoughts too buried

Hush my love

You moan too loudly

Alien thing

This hand is strange
it doesn't belong in the same vein it did before
remember the beauty of veins
attached to wrist attached to *thing*
as they protruded violet hued and
swollen after being wrung out, probed and punctured
for the little blood that could be found
longing to be discovered and
I remind myself that the *thing* is attached to my arm
my shoulder and useless limb
does not end there
I am reminded that this *thing* is a gift
to learn to use this part of me again
-not unlike a toddler-
is some kind of beautiful - apparently
it does not feel that way
it does not feel the same as the other
both in mind and body
I am congratulated for lifting the kettle
with the *thing*
even when only a quarter full
it is more of an achievement
to use it
to bring a Bulmers to my lips
and glug down
glug it away
slow steady but I am not winning

texting is painstakingly slow with only one
a birthday card laboriously poured over
I cannot use it like you can
tapping your nails on any and every surface
until I am retching green with resentment
"But you're practically ambidextrous!!!!!"
No. I'm not.
I am patiently awaiting the day it takes a part away from me
not so much patiently as anxiously
the hat tricks are tricky
the dread created beside the green table
the *thing* shakes as it clutches the stick
this is the trauma that is loud and proud
out in the open for all to see
other dregs lie just beneath the surface
when you break through
it is even messier than a hand that doesn't do the job

A stranger

But not quite strange
Enough
And there are no happy endings
Absolutely none
Not a single one
What am I doing
I cannot be happy
Surely
Am I ill
Why is my heart beating so
It hammered out of my chest
The day your lips touched me
I touched you more like
It feels scary
But not risky
The lack of risk makes me question things
Things you say
Under my lips are yours
Lips on fire
Hotter than live wire
Still
I do not understand you
You tell me you like me
I do not believe you
How can I
When you do not talk to me
But you did write a song

About me
Called lonely

I feel lonely
How is that possible
With 2 people to talk to

Untitled 1

You smelled of new cigarettes and old leather
The epitome of a lone wanderer
When you fucked me you didn't quite look
Or at least you didn't see
In the morning bleary-eyed and bushy-tailed
I descended
And you didn't stop me
Then you told me you didn't want to lose me

As a friend

Untitled 2

I wrote enough poetry about you
In order to not know you
At all
I wanted to write a poetry book about you
But then I thought
Fuck you
But then I thought
I'll do it anyway
Though it's about you
It's *for* ME
AND THEN IT WAS HARDLY ABOUT YOU ANYWAY

You made me feel like a mug
So
I'm reclaiming my mug

hehe

Boring

Sat on the bus in my fishnets

Waiting for my pills to kick in

Feeling a bit sick

There's a man crossing the road with a plant taller than him

You just got rejected

Unfortunately regrettably sadly:
- We are writing to inform you
- On this occasion we are not able to offer you
- You did not make the final selection
- We will not be taking your application
- This is a courtesy message (Just to let you know)
- On this occasion
- This is yet another rejection
- It was a particularly tough decision

Unfortunately

Unfortunately

Unfortunately

Sorry
- Although, sadly, we cannot move forward
- It did make our long list!

Frustrated shouting screaming swearword fhsghfj^%hsg

- We were thrilled to read and receive it
- What?!
- Your application has not been shortlisted
- We do hope you will be interested
- We do hope that you will continue to write (While we will not)
  We know that rejections play a part in life

  We want to reiterate

- The quality and amount of applications

Thanks for rubbing it in

Thanks for the confirmation
I mean–
Unfortunately

- Again, we are sorry to be emailing with this news
- We appreciate the time and energy you put into applying for the brief

Blood
Sweat
Tears
And grief

ERROR Address not found
ERROR Message not delivered
Crowned the queen of rejection
Even my emails are being rejected
Not that it's affected me
 or anything
    - We know that rejection plays a part in this life
Spoken like a true pocket-knife

Places were:
    - Limited
Decisions were:
    - Tough
And other stuff
To that effect

You were:
    - Unsuccessful

- Not selected
- Not included

Not taken forward
- Not able
- Different direction
- Let's leave it for now
- We're going to pass
- We quite enjoyed your tape

A slap in the face
Or maybe I'm just bitter
That I'm not a winner
Or maybe I'm just bored
At another round of 'not taken onboard'
- On this occasion
- Unfortunately
- We were impressed with your proposal
- On this occasion
- UNFORTUNATELY
- We will keep you in mind for the future
- sorry
- Unfortunately
- Never to be heard from again

ROMP
(Originally performed as part of Does My Fanny Look Big in This?)

Does it make you feel emasculated?
I'm just trying to feel less irritated
Beneath sexually frustrated
Why does it leave you devastated?
When I'm just fucking LIBERATED
You: humiliated
Me: exhilarated
With my body you've many a time masturbated
So allow me the vibrations I've long since awaited
You don't want to go in there not lubricated
It's a sure way to keep me motivated
Titillated illuminated accelerated
And that can only be good for you too
I'm infatuated

With my clit sucker

You're boring

Sleepless

Sleep evaded me as a child
My mind perhaps
Too full to dream
No space for anything more
More than anything
I wanted to sink into that nothingness
Occasionally
 The blueberry man visited me
I fell down many a hole
With no rabbits to be seen
Just awake
And waking
And ceiling
I was given a tape of lullabies
At an age far beyond
All I could fathom
While that delicate music was
Played
Was the amount of time I had been awake
The last track a melody of doom
So I left my room
Cried on the stairs instead
Crying out I didn't want to be dead

Until my mum came up to carry me back
And the cycle repeated
This persisted nightly
Until
My grandmother
Sleeping beside me
 Where my granddad Used to
Of her own free will
Shushed me
And soothed me with a single line
You don't need to sleep
You just need to rest
And I shut my agitated eyes
For the final time
In hospital
I slept all the time
Never quite achieving rest
If only you could store sleep
Like memories
But they evade me too
A quiet corner in the uni library
With blankets and cushions and
Peace For me to nap my worries away
But they always seem to stay
Hang around until waking

Nowadays

Sleep is a funny thing

We have a strange relationship

I sleep on trains

But am still a light sleeper

There is such thing as too long a nap

The hours my head hits the pillow are in delicate balance

Delicate

Like my head

Sleep evades me

Like my fragility

Bare
(Originally published in The Unpublishable Zine)

you picked up a 3 quid bunch of wilting flowers from the flimsy hut by the side of the road. they swept away my resentment and turned me soft and lovely again. they died 2 days later. they were already dead. I am an ode to all things delicate and easy, the way the petal curls makes me creamy. the way you grunt in bed curls the downy hair between my thighs. I could curl away from you in the same manner, but then you would know, magicians should not reveal their secrets; too soon anyway. the baby pink of the tulips match my peach fuzzed cheeks as you spend another hour glued to your phone.

roses are not the only thorns

I am told that flowers are beautiful/I am told that I am beautiful/by the men/therefore I know these things to be true/the words are ugly in my mouth as I try relentlessly to taste them/much like the blossom that does not appease but I steadily continue to chew

#1 of #2

I need to speak to someone
At all times
To prove that I can
To prove that
I am
You didn't do anything wrong
As such
Except for
Not being him

Thought I was boring
Until I came across you
You were still fit though
And told me you missed me
Kissed me
And gave me a card with a bee
'I hope your director is nice to you.'
(He definitely wasn't)

I thought that was all I needed
How could you miss me
When you didn't know the first thing about me
Nor me about you
Thought we might learn together
I got bored with waiting

Bye bye flowerpot man #1

The sex was fun while it lasted
Though it didn't last long
That's how I like it
You were boring
But I was still sad when you stopped messaging
Another person forgetting
Clearly I'm boring and forgettable
But surely
Not as much as you

square peg

Confusion
Confusion engulfs me
Wracking up, a sweat
Invades my shivering body
I know what I want
At least
I am forcing you into that want-shaped hole
Just as you force yourself into me
I want you to
After all
It's easier that way
Not as much to say
Explain
Explain to me
How on paper you're perfect
But (not) in reality
Is perfection too fucking easy

Hum (in my) Drum

I have become obsessed with mundanities
You at the hob cooking dinner is unbelievably sexy
Hearing you read to me
Before we drift gently off to sleep
Sets my soul alight
Sitting on the sofa perched against your knees
Watching shitty tv
Is my favourite pastime
I could sit in front of you
in a lukewarm bath for hours
drinking a lukewarm cup of tea
I live for a cuddle and a quickie
     -not the adventurous kind
But I'd absolutely take that too
asking me what I want for breakfast sarcastically
when we both know
there's only one gluten free option
anxious conversations that require your rationality
yes you always approach diplomatically
enough to make me swoon
washing the pots while I wink at you in the window
arouses me illogically
searching for you in the night absentmindedly
when we part ways of touching
get me going automatically

      - there's beauty in banality

Untitled 3

Tiktok trend of strangulation ???
Only go there for validation
A 27 year old seeking affirmation
I fear profusely
For the teenage population

Untitled 4

The most tedious
persistent
soundtrack to my life
have you taken your meds ???
played on infinite repeat

Untitled 5

1 day off is nice
But there's always work to be done
2 days off and I'm ticking one by one
3 days off and I'm not having much fun
4 days off and I'm fucking undone
5 days off and I'm adding to my list
6 days off- risk of dying bored persists
7 hfgdhndjfjtnd@@@!!!- you get the gist

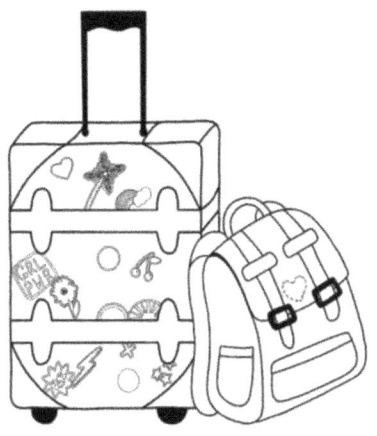

Travelling

The smell of rain invades
Makes me feel dirty
I bask in the dirtiness
Everything is sensory
Everything is overwhelming
When in Rome!

                              -EDIT: I didn't go to Rome

Mardy Bum

(Originally *published* in Greenteeth Press's Yorkshire Anthology)

OK, OK. So you're not from New York City. You're from Rotherham, but that's really not a problem, that's not so bad. Rotherham was probably the best night out I ever had. For us, cheesy chips and gravy is no passing fad. Hiya and welcome to the part of the country where you natter to strangers on the bus as if they were your Dad.

Being Northern means being friendly, being a right good mate. It's not surprising really that everyone "wants to live like common people." We're first rate. Where nights out are dedicated to getting in a first-rate state but that's not without effort- we aren't bloody lightweights. A scrap that you'll instigate will escalate but rarely devastate when it quickly ends in a hand shake or a gruff "good one mate," and the tension dissipates quicker than it came. Plus - we dish out and give out just as much love, but you will get called a cop-out if you have another hooch love. Don't be surprised if your friendly northern pal urinates in a questionable place while 'ammered. This simply illustrates and demonstrates their dominance and place in the family of primates. Northerners love a pint more than I would dare to say, I mean, I could easily talk to you about my love of a bev for more than a day- and that's OK! Also, the price in the North probably explains why we get so carried away.

Here's 3 tips to do it the northern way.

Number 1. Mopping up your gravy with a bread slice after finishing your Yorkshire pud, is practically gourmet.

Number 2. A ginnel or jennel means an alleyway.

Number 3. When I say "ey up" or "nah then" I am actually asking "how goes the day?"

Don't get me started on the debate that is bread. When you can call it something as cool as a bread cake, why would you call it anything else instead? Roll, bap, barm, cob, batch; those are all dead. We're strict about our bread, but we're stricter about our brews. Milk and one, builders and cuppa are the terms you've got to use. You're a mardy bum or a pillock if you don't thank the bus driver, and did I mention you can get two pints in Spoons for under a fiver? The weather isn't cold - it's fresh and we're tough in the rain and wind, not nesh. We use swear words and flat caps to address problems close to our heart, and we delight in *Pete McKee's* various works of art. We'll put you at ease, we aren't afraid to get down on our knees... to scrub. We say it's High Green mate via Hillsborough, please.

We are the children born of these industrial towns, where the metal and the steel fit together to make up our vast playgrounds. Marvel in the diverse noises and city sounds, the flickering lights and hustle and bustle of this busy place as you turn in awe around and around. Then you're travelling round a corner and the city scape is no more. You're walking and walking. For northerners a walk is like a kid finding themselves in a candy store. You're climbing over rolling hills of The Peak District and making your feet sore, but you ignore it, for there is so much incredible land to find. Explore it. Discover the great outdoors. The north is somewhere you're sure to fall for and stand for. It'll cause an uproar inside you. It's not just somewhere to make do, pass through- it's somewhere to pursue, aspire to, run to. And you do.

Whether it's reyt good or right good, *Liam Gallagher* or *Alex Turner*, *Pulp* or *The Stone Roses*, if you're northern, you'll be at the pub until it closes. Being too amazing is the problem northern heritage poses and then you'll get all cocky and write a shitty spoken word piece that doesn't rhyme. *PAUSE* Eating fish and chips by the beach is our favourite pastime, at meal times or any time really. We drench everything in *Hendo's* freely. Yep, us northerners are reyt greedy. *Greggs* runs through my veins and I'm proud, I'm just all cooped up in my own little northern cloud. You can hear our accent coming for miles around when we're in a crowd, well yeah, we're a little bit loud but we're northern and proud.

We know what poverty looks like but we also look out for each other, protect one another, treat others as though they're your father or mother. We are proud of our roots and we wear our sturdy *Dr Marten* boots with pride too. In the North of England we grew into what we are now, and somehow the north will stay within us for as long as we allow.

Blissful ignorance

I have lost so much touch
Here let me show you
I am not worldly wise
I know that as Edinburgh feels close to home
We are in a different country
Yet it feels just around the corner
I fell asleep on the train and then I was in Doncaster
It was more difficult to get from there to Chapeltown than Scotland to England
I am not very observant
I hardly notice the stench of the overflowing bins
Only paying attention
To place my banana skin precariously on the top of Waste Mountain
I receive reports of the fringe accommodation prices rising
And feel fortunate that I haven't had to pay
this time

Going higher

I have moved from Sheffield to Leeds
And that in itself is not unusual
I moved from Sheffield to Cornwall for uni
That was slightly more inconceivable
The independence it provides is slightly more
Bizarre
Slightly more
delicious
I wander these red-brick neighbourhoods with
Anticipation
Seldom more inebriation
Yet everything to play for
Possibilities endless
I am closer and altogether further away
A mobile free library around every bend
Possibilities endless
Arcadia; the pub with good games
And a friend
With a friend
Possibilities endless
The gym a short walk away
Charity shops full of gems
Possibilities endless
You- 10 minutes down the road
Endless possibilities
When I first moved here everything looked
The same

I was lost
Scared
Endless streets
Now I live here and everything looks
The same
Number 79
Slightly more
And I am
Home

Apart

For the first time
I didn't feel
Joy
Elation
Bliss
I felt scared
Give me those feelings back
A job is a job
BUT
If I wanted more money for a lot less
I could work at a car wash
Not sell my soul to the devil

You've never known anxiety until //

You attend a stand-up gig alone at the Edinburgh fringe in a grotty cave and have to wait for a considerable period before it starts, as you were stupid and used to getting to performances half an hour in advance, what is this 5 minute turn around fuckery?

You've never known the fringe until //

You run from show to show with no time to process the dramatic, tragic display of something you aren't sure is verging on paedophilia, but you can bet you're going to run into the venue next door and watch hot-clown sex

You've never known hot-clown-sex until //

Your orgasm is so good you start to think it couldn't possibly have been inflicted by this clown laying haphazardly on top of you. Yes, you are correct, it wasn't the clown, it was your vibrator

You've never known orgasms until //

You've tried a clit sucker called ro-

You've never felt like such a sucker until //

You kid yourself that it's a good idea to go watch a musical about sexual assault and sit on the front row and spend all the time you don't have unpacking it wondering how they could have made it at all - despite your own experiences that you still have to deal with but are avoiding at any cost BLURGH

You've never known joy until //

You watch a Japanese puppet show with accompanying cello and belly laugh/ literally almost fall off your chair lol'ing and the performers look so happy I think I might have to cry a little to appreciate their full potential

The artist that knows

You painted the city - a reimagined art form
With metal cans rattling like chattering teeth
Lining every spare surface inside your humble abode
That isn't covered in the art itself
Inside the city
That in turn held you above it
I want to plaster the stickers you gave me with your name on
and the ones that said
open your eyes to tory lies
All over my body
Over my mouth so I cannot put my foot in it
Over my foot so I too can be lifted
This time
By you

You call countless other people "your man"
I know I am not included
In that elusive club
Let   me   in
Wow
to be one of your men

You say
Take a day for you

I protest

    This is all for me

you see right through me
you stare at me for too long

I break
        What the fuck do you know about me

You only know the city
Not the galaxy
I almost break the façade
Don't do that
You can't look at me
Because you might see

Who was I kidding
You already knew
                            - The fool

I had a lot of time but at the same time no time at all

I plot out a potential life in this city in my head in this city in my head / I watch the sunset on Arthurs Seat and we dance and laugh and drink and smoke and dance some more (why the fuck did I turn the dancing down) until the sun rises on said seat / we topple down head first gathering human bodies as we go so we are a mass of amiable pals / genial friends tumbling downwards in a ball of flesh and sweat and mud that is grinning from ear to ear somehow / fringing off the friendliest people you will ever meet! / no, serious / but not severely at all / we all go home for strawberry smoothie with salty cream (perhaps boring but no doubt best) / not for long though as we need our culture-catch desperately / we are hungry for it (hungrier than for the salty cream) / but we won't slurp in front of the cast while they perform as that would be rude / 6am and we are running for the bus that won't come in approximately 43 minutes / taxi is 32 then 15 then 20 then 31 then at last it settles at 32 / Now drinks !! and ket !!! / I am stumbling / on less drinks the next night I am A OK / if only the house prices weren't extortionate and my Scottish accent was half decent / maybe I could stay

London 1 and 2

In this BIG city I feel small
I have been picking my fingers constantly
I've been considering shagging someone much older than me
On the tube and my huge stickered case bashes into me
Only 4 stops to go
I have a brownie waiting in my bag
Gf of course
In this strange city I feel a bit like the brownie
Neglected at the bottom of a paper bag
Surrounded by items
More useful - more consumable
Even the hairbrush

In this acclaimed city I feel insignificant
But I doubt I ever was
Significant
So what's a change in city
When you're feeling small anyway
                You need to take a chill pill
                You need to calm down
You need to take any pill
And get out of this town

Leeds 1 and 2

Tonight I went on my first Leeds date:
I was home - makeup off before 11
I considered asking him inside
Not because I wanted to
But for something to do
Because that's just what you do
But I didn't
I think this is called – growth?

Date no 2 led to:
living out of my backpack
My back pain is intense
Belongings squashed side by side
(Is there a brick in there?)
I make my way
Past the fluorescent lights
Of Headingley stadium for the millionth time
For you darling, anything
I'll bring it all
The kitchen sink

Birmingham 1 and 2

Surrounded by cool ass people
Feeling so uncomfortably aloooooooone

Why is alone so uncomfortable anyway
Why do people always ask you if you're doing OK?
The pub looked cool
So I thought I'd sit for one or two
Offers of company
Rejected
To chat to the bar staff
Especially the one in the cool striped jumper
-I told you so
-You asked my number
(I thought you might like me)
-You appeared edgy and dangerous
(God knows how I appeared)
-I helped you clean the bar
-I stayed for staff lock-in
-I kissed you on the cheek
-I got dropped off home
          You told me you had a gf

Time goes by so slowly
When you aren't performing a show at quarter to 11 at night
The night is your oyster
There's nothing to do
I'm glad I didn't wash my hair for you not to turn up
I'm gonna go home for food and bojack
The difference in nights is startling

Oh York oh York

Place of breathtaking beauty and
More importantly maybe
Breathtaking pubs
I see your yorvik centre
Full of mannequins
And I raise you my
York dungeons
Full of living breathing actors
Purple hued low lying whispy clouds
Streak across the sky
As I leave work
Almost but not quite
In darkness yet again
The cobbles and ghostly tales hold musings
Of a time long ago
But relate closer to the time now
More than I could possibly imagine
If only I had a day to meander in their footsteps..

But I have no time!
        Endless time !
                Yet no time at all !!

The Vikings are after me

People of Edinburgh that made an impression

Nemo, not the fish - the fool
The rain and bananas and painted metal
I wish I'd kept your jumper so I had physical evidence
Lindsay, always smiling
The loveliest, happiest strawberry blonde human I ever did see
Jack, a scotsboy not a scotsman
You're fit as fuck and I'm high as a kite
The drugs actually made you more subdued
Z- Romona Flowers vibes
Allie- too cool to be so young
Heps- Wise beyond her years
Alex- a dog that is a cat is lovely
Terry- so good to be true
Taio- holds the future in his hands
Merrill- means well and does better
James- is a middle aged man flirting with me / or is he gay
Linda- effortlessly cool and even more beautiful / am I gay
EDIT: yes
Ollie- I like your haircut
Callie- the best of us
Could I have really made so many friends
Or were you all conceived inside my head

A cream place called home

The walls are ivory and sparse as this is one home that hasn't been populated for long

in the long line of homes that won't be lived in long but loved nonetheless

The wide stance of an elephant stomps down the stairs ready to pounce on

A new mother and father sit atop a barely unwrapped settee waiting

They are so naïve and beautiful and naïve

They are not aware of the elephant

Well they might be a little

They know little of what is to come

Reverse it

The walls are ivory and sparse but littered with memories from previous tenants

A little girl bounds down the steep stairs with all the grace of an elephant, she is giggling and carefree

She is happy

She is so happy

Nothing has ever caused her to not be happy

The people at the bottom waiting patiently know this

Are all too aware of this

They want to protect her

But how do you do this

The world is full of poachers

And they are so naïve

But beautiful
"Ellie"
"Is that an elephant I hear?"
A giggle reverberates around the walls of the room
And they welcome her into their arms
She will be safe for now

Loving

I relate my life to sex and the city
Much more frequently
Than I'd like to

But not just the sex
The city
And the friends
And the strange situations

Sex and the city
Gets me

Let's go girls

The best thing about being a woman is you can call yourself a woman and you're done. That's literally it, you call yourself a woman: you are a woman. Same for a man but we're talking about women here.

 Other amazing things about being a woman besides the prerogative to have a little fun: we have mastered the art of communication. We can literally tell from one short glance that our fellow sister is in trouble and will get her a phone and a taxi in a heartbeat. This unspoken language between us is known as girlspeak and it's written into our DNA. So if you ever have the cheek to cross one of us we'll be plotting and discussing our revenge while we are 'taking a leak'.

Passing a tampon in the bog is like passing a baton in a race, it's practically the same as an 'I love you, you're worth so much more' text or even a warm wine fuelled embrace. And it sucks that we still have to go out at night in pairs and we have to say we're in a relationship with our best gal so we don't get harassed at all but never have I had more fun that on a girly pub crawl in those pairs or on a 3 hour long phone call with my bestie. If you're thick enough to catcall us after night fall when we're together just be prepared for our mic drop, it's not called girl power for nothing after all.

I'm going out tonight, I'm feeling alright but then I get catcalled. Catcalling should be reserved for cats - you just want to get a reaction out of us and probably will but you should know catcalling is the perfect indicator to point out to us the arse holes. In a roundabout way you're doing us a favour because now we don't have to pretend to be nice to you. Being a woman is telling your girl friends to text you when they get home. You want to do it and you're happy to but the fact you have to is like having unfortunate irritable bowel syndrome.

Oh woah oh oh go totally crazy because Women live 2-3 years longer than men - I wonder how I can fill those extra years, maybe with inventing a tool that allows us not to need men. Oh wait. Women wrote the most successful book series of our time; we've got a lot of important stuff to say. It's what makes us so fantastic in a debate. We have to work harder than men but that's OK because we are bloody strong, anyone who states otherwise is absolutely bloody wrong. Being a woman is not defined by your spouse, partner or lack thereof. It literally makes no difference whether it's another person or yourself for whom you fell in love. Nor is it defined by your ability to bear a child. You are a woman if you are a mother, were once a mother or have not and will never be a mother.

 No inhibitions, make no conditions. Don't let your self-worth or opinion of yourself be swayed by another. I completely understand that I own a great deal of privilege being assigned the gender I am at birth and I am also lucky that I am beginning to come to terms with my own worth. If you're not there yet that's OK, what is it they say? Rome wasn't built in a day. And women are even more beautiful and magical than Rome so it'll probably take even longer than that.

Men's shirts short skirts. Short skirts, long skirts, trousers, shorts, pants, no skirts and polos, v-necks, bras, t shirts, crop tops, vests or work shirts. They rock every god damn one and none make you more of a women or a better woman than anyone else. Your specific body parts don't have any say over whether you're a woman. Sorry gals, having breasts or a vagina don't automatically make you one. One is not born, but becomes a woman - Simone De

Beauvoir - Say it louder for the people in the back we cheer!

Man I feel like a woman and being a woman can be as feminine or as masculine as you like – don't like my gender expression take a hike! I know it's not as easy as that for some women and men though and I can only hope that people become more aware and accepting and those who still dislike it get on their bike.

Colour your hair, do what you dare! laughing together, drinking together (cocktails or coffee), crying together and them telling you 'you can do so much better' and deep down you knowing you are an absolute treasure, supporting whomever just because she is one of you, being strong and brave and beautiful forever. Being a woman is…anything. There is no specific way to be a woman. It's your womanhood, own it and don't let anyone tell you shit otherwise. Being a woman is pretty awesome. Beyonce is a woman, I rest my case.

Gathering
(originally published in SouthChild Lit)

milk teeth in an empty marmalade jar on the table top
euphoric relief that they are still sleeping
watch closely as their eyelids flutter gently
seaweed gently swaying in an ocean bed
another bed
this one is just as unfamiliar
but strangely
a sense of belonging
consider for a second taking their hand
the soft sensation (memory) of palm on palm
        gathers you
regain control
gather your things and steal away

half way down the alien street you falter
did you forget-
yes
you summon courage from the pit
march back to the pebble dash speckled home
coming face to face with sunshine
a milky tea stretched out towards you
at the door

Recipe for a reyt good day out

Pick a day in the height of summer that is bound to be really hot in the afternoon but turn chilly in the evening / Dress in a skimpy floral number and bring a baggy, battered band jumper with you- add a flower crown and glitter if you're feeling extra extra / pack a Tupperware of packet pasta that you rush and nearly burn right before heading out the door / Pick your best, most fun friend and invite them along for the ride (what a ride it's going to be an'all) / stroll down to the local supermarket in your chunky docs and pay for 3 2 litre bottles of the cheapest, nastiest cider you can get your hands on (1 and a half bottles each) -and maybe a packet of crisps / make a beeline for your closest northern park with a dodgy hill and lots of trees to have a not so discreet wee behind / set up camp near a log you can perch on (you'll mostly end up rolling around on the floor if we're being honest) / take numerous videos with silly filters, chugging the filth but most importantly hugging and kissing each other because that's what best friends in their late teens do / talk for hours about everything and nothing and a bit of shit on the side / pee at free will when it suits- laugh at each other's squats and compare lengths of bushes / eat the now cold pasta hungrily and messily / throw said pasta back up and all over your docs after drinking approximately 2.3 litres of the dirty liquid / when it gets a little dark- blast out your favourite pop-punk tunes and DANCE / confess your best friend status for only the 17th time this evening / fall in the sick a little / stagger home at half 10 so you can see your parents before they go to bed but not before promising you'll do it all again next week and taking a sloppy picture with flash that shows off your bright blue hair and toothy grin

But it never did happen again, quite like that. If only we could go back to 17. I'd even take 16 and we both know how shit that was.

SPL IT

I am always splitting things
a few examples:
- My nose

Helter skelter down stone steps
- My chin

My tolerance was even less when I got out of hospital
- The bone of my ankle

The trampoline, of course
- My tooth

Another drunken mishap
- My head

The old bike story again
- Another girl's head

I was trying to kiss her
>(pretty sure that needs unpacking)
- My head

On the wall of a strangers house while intoxicated and not wanting to be touched but touching anyway
- My head

You'd think a brain injury would make you more careful
- My hymen

I always had heavy periods
- Relationships

I am impulsive to a fault
- Friendships

I will love you perhaps too much
- My heart

Like I said, I love too deep. It's as much my fault as yours
- My head
Are you getting the picture

I can put things back together too
Though I am not as good at that
I mainly leave it to the doctors
They are trained after all

Strange behaviour

We spit it out gleefully
- Because men only buy you a drink with an ulterior motive
- Because I don't trust any of my drinks alone
- Because I've heard the rumours about that bar anyway
- Because I've lost track of the times I've been sexually harassed
- Because I have to feign a fake phonecall
- Because I don't want to walk on the same side of the street
- Because I've blocked out of my brain all the catcalls I've experienced
- Because apparently it was my fault though how and why I do not know
- Because I had to pay thousands of pounds to try and raise the necessary awareness
- Because you always have a friend with a horror story

Or you are the friend

Strange behaviour (?)

Fucked up more like

But we laugh it off

Or we would burst into tears

Failing that

We would B U R S T

Meet me in the pumpkin patch

Burnt sienna makes my eyes pop
And pop they do and oh so
Gargoyle like you clutch me
Clutch me tighter dear
Oh dear
I got a little too excited by the
Home sense Halloween candle collection
the spiced latte essence
the apple cider effervescence
the frickin' bats exciting adolescents
the witches brew
and you
when I recalled the encounter
got a little scared
slightly disturbed
by my crazed enthusiasm
But laughed along anyway
I let out a cackle
I am going to perform as a witch in a play
I always wanted to be dunked live on stage
Til then let us roll in the pumpkin
Patch
And we'll carve our own faces into our own bulbous heads
Sickly sweet smiles replacing garish grins
You are my magic wand my enrapturing web
Me your princess
You my pumpkin

Learn and remember

You can tell them to stay
as much as you like
force it down their throat
until they choke
because you're choking
at the thought of being alone
but they remain choking
then they really choke
it has the reverse effect
than the one you want

I can't remember you as anything other than
I don't know you anymore
therefore I cannot remember
how easy it was to reach out for your hand
and touch it to my face
how easily I love you
dripped from my bones
tripped off your tongue
how easy it was for me to fall
                       How easy my heart to break
          How easy
     I was

We go to Tenerife in under a month

My hair is greasy again
I washed it yesterday
Too much sex
Is that a thing?

It took work
But after such an easy ride
Came grinding to a halt
I needed to see someone else put in the effort
Along with myself
To remind me I wasn't the only one at fault

You weren't on insta
I couldn't stalk you
Couldn't do my research
A sort of creepy animalistic ritual to go through
You remained a mystery
And I desire to be mystified

Snuggly in a lumpy bed like the porridge you chew
Just another 17 kisses
Mouth a third full
Continue to chew

I was always certain of you
And you proved me wrong
With *you* I'm never sure

But I'll hold my tongue

I have to
Because I've been mistaken before
And though I don't like it at all
I'll be mistaken perhaps once more

I'm waiting for our holiday
In more ways than one
I'm anxiously awaiting
The coming undone

Kittens

you couldn't separate us to go to the loo
we chain smoked for something for our hands to do
we fell over and over and
over again
mainly me but you could be a bad friend
glittery cactus jacks and sourz shots !!
sitting on stranger's knees and sofa cots
sunlight first kiss wasn't so much a kiss as a rip roaring bleary eyed
HELLO
    Oh no
I didn't remove my makeup
    Oh no
It's way past time for me to wake up
I should go
but   NO
I have leftover pizza
and
some sort of form of self-inflicted amnesia
so I'll traipse home around quarter to 3
wearing last nights barely there dress
complete with #ohsotrendy cut on knee
And we'll message and debrief for days to come
Until the next time we get to parade
our 16 year old disposable income

10 years down the line your lack of income clings to those #memories

Baff

Moments treasured in luke warm baths
If I had a bath
I do now
Fill it with the shower
Shower in a bath
Always good for a laugh
You shared my first with me
It was cold but altogether divine (not unlike us)
Let's spend that time all the time
Most of the time we're just listening to each other whine
In the bedroom
at the table
Me about my life
You about life
Your intelligence is so fucking sexy
You intimidate me
Sext me xxx

Untitled 6

I'm playing my happy playlist on Spotify for the first time in months

I usually pick moody

It represents my personality

Now – so does happy

Untitled 7

I couldn't remember the word for self-love
Waterstones is that for me anyway

Or even better-
A dirty, run down, ramshackle store that's home to a mysterious collection of paper strewn together

- *Books - The real love of my life*

Untitled 8

A stranger drew us
- not once

But twice
We were presented with the finished article

That was the very first time

We saw each other together
Before we'd even seen each other
He said we looked happy
We didn't know yet if we could be

Untitled 9

"I think I'm falling in love with you"
You only think?
I fell in love with you the night we met
Take me back to the night we met
>You locking us out of my room
>When I only wanted to go to the kitchen to
>Wash 2 pots
>We dry humped and waited for the locksmith on the sofa
>Glorious and much anticipated relief
>When we (you) entered at last

But I do fall in love as easy as I fall down the stairs
And I'm clumsy in the extreme
But this time it feels different
>It always does

What if I pretend to be bored?
Maybe I'll get away with indifference
Who the fuck are you kidding
>You're not that good of an actor mate

In another life you squeezed me out to fill out the donuts

The cobbled streets and dusty pavements lead the way to a distantly familiar home
With pebbledashed foundations and a gnome on a swing hanging from a crooked tree
Or was that a memory? A dream?
Let's call it both
I don't see the resemblance   but I know it's there
Even in photographs it doesn't seem likely
But still -
We would be the best of friends
Or strangers   nowhere in between
                I smile at you outside class
In the park
                Just behind the donut factory
Where you supplied the insides of those sugary treats
And taught yourself
Willpower
That you promptly unlearnt
        You blink blankly
       You don't understand me
  Like so many of your lessons
That Granddad had no patience with you over
                Why do you insist on following me?

But then   a flicker
A thing vaguely resembling recognition flashes across

A connection
            Existing only through a period of living inside
another
      Making your home there
I am now just a twinkle
we *would* be best friends
Or strangers
Nowhere
Else
It doesn't end
At the cutting of the squishy thread
            Unlike a hermit
                  I wouldn't change my shell

Acknowledgements

to my friends and family who populate this book: ha – gotcha!

to ben: thanks for being the dreamiest muse I could never do justice in writing.

to my health: thanks for keeping me on my toes (and fuck you.)

to Sheffield Theatres: thanks for growing me up reyt good and proper and later believing in my work (and me.)

to mama, nannan and granddad: thanks for being my no1 fans, always. Love you x

to the 3 J's: thanks for everything xxx

Warmest

Ellie

Other anthologies and collections available from Stairwell Books

Goldfish	Jonathan Aylett
Strike	Sarah Wimbush
Marginalia	Doreen Hinchliffe
The Estuary and the Sea	Jennifer Keevill
In | Between	Angela Arnold
Quiet Flows the Hull	Clint Wastling
Lunch on a Green Ledge	Stella Davis
there is an england	Harry Gallagher
Iconic Tattoo	Richard Harries
Herdsmenization	Ngozi Olivia Osuoha
On the Other Side of the Beach, Light	Daniel Skyle
Words from a Distance	Ed. Amina Alyal, Judi Sissons
Fractured	Shannon O'Neill
Unknown	Anna Rose James, Elizabeth Chadwick Pywell
When We Wake We Think We're Whalers from Eden	Bob Beagrie
Awakening	Richard Harries
Starspin	Graehame Barrasford Young
A Stray Dog, Following	Greg Quiery
Blue Saxophone	Rosemary Palmeira
Steel Tipped Snowflakes 1	Izzy Rhiannon Jones, Becca Miles, Laura Voivodeship
Where the Hares Are	John Gilham
The Glass King	Gary Allen
Gooseberries	Val Horner
Poetry for the Newly Single 40 Something	Maria Stephenson
Northern Lights	Harry Gallagher
Lodestone	Hannah Stone
Learning to Breathe	John Gilham
Throwing Mother in the Skip	William Thirsk-Gaskill
New Crops from Old Fields	Ed. Oz Hardwick
The Ordinariness of Parrots	Amina Alyal
Homeless	Ed. Ross Raisin
Somewhere Else	Don Walls
Taking the Long Way Home	Steve Nash

For further information please contact rose@stairwellbooks.com

www.stairwellbooks.co.uk
@stairwellbooks

www.ingramcontent.com/pod-product-compliance
Ingram Content Group UK Ltd.
Pitfield, Milton Keynes, MK11 3LW, UK
UKHW040246170225
455194UK00001BA/17